$4.99

E
419
Bo

Bove, Linda
     Sesame Street
sign language ABC
with Linda Bove

DATE DUE

MY 0 2 '88	JUN 0 2 95	
JE 0 1 '88	JAN 3 1 96	
JF 15 '88	FEB 0 7 97	
SE 7 8	FEB 2 0 97	
SE 25 '89	NOV 2 4 97	
JE 20 '90	OC 12 99	
JA 31 '9	JA 10 '00	
MR 9 '91	JY 05 01	
SE 26 '91	AG 02 01	
SE 1 '92	JY 31 06	
MY 1 5 '93	JY 22 10	
APR 1 0 95		

NOTE TO PARENTS

Sign language is a beautiful and expressive way to communicate which both children and adults will find intriguing. <u>Sesame Street Sign Language ABC with Linda Bove</u> is an exciting introduction to sign language. Photographs show Linda Bove demonstrating the sign for each letter of the alphabet and more than 75 useful words. Illustrations of the Sesame Street Muppets depict the words signed on that page. With the words in this book, children can have fun forming simple sentences in sign language.

ABOUT LINDA BOVE

Linda Bove is an actress who is deaf. She has been sharing her signing and theatrical talents with the television viewers of <u>Sesame Street</u> for many years as a cast member. She has also been seen in the movie <u>Sesame Street Presents: Follow That Bird!</u> and played the lead in the road show of <u>Children of a Lesser God</u>. She is also the author of <u>Sesame Street Sign Language Fun</u>, a book many children will want to go on to after this lively introduction.

SESAME STREET

Sign Language ABC
with Linda Bove

A Random House PICTUREBACK®

Copyright © 1985 Children's Television Workshop. Sesame Street MUPPETS © Muppets, Inc. 1985. All rights reserved under International and Pan-American Copyright Conventions. ® Sesame Street and the Sesame Street sign are trademarks and service marks of the Children's Television Workshop. Published in the United States by Random House, Inc., New York, and simultaneously in Canada by Random House of Canada Limited, Toronto, in conjunction with the Children's Television Workshop.

Library of Congress Cataloging in Publication Data: Bove, Linda. Sesame Street sign language ABC with Linda Bove. SUMMARY: The residents of Sesame Street introduce the letters of the alphabet both in sign language and through pictures. 1. Sign language—Juvenile literature. 2. English language—Alphabet—Juvenile literature. [1. Alphabet. 2. Sign language] I. Shevett, Anita, ill. II. Shevett, Steve, ill. III. Cooke, Tom, ill. IV. Title. HV2480.B68   1985   419   [E]   85-1845   ISBN: 0-394-87516-8 (trade); 0-394-97516-2 (lib. bdg.)

Manufactured in the United States of America   2 3 4 5 6 7 8 9 0

Sign Language ABC
with Linda Bove

I   love   you !

illustrated by Tom Cooke
photographs by Anita and Steve Shevett

FEATURING JIM HENSON'S SESAME STREET MUPPETS

Random House / Children's Television Workshop

Hello!

My

name

is

Linda.

Follow

me

and

learn

your

A

B

C's!

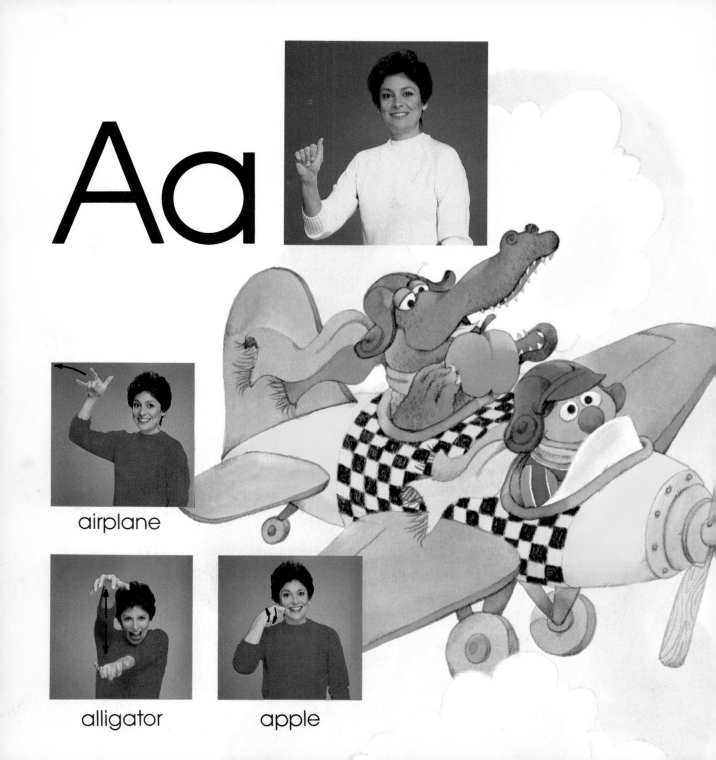

Aa

airplane

alligator

apple

Bb

book

big

bird

Cc

car

cat

clown

Dd

Where   **is**   **my**   **duck?**

Ee

elephant

eye

elevator

Ff

flag

fox

fence

Gg

girl

grouch

guitar

Hh

Happy   birthday,   hippopotamus!

Ii

I   love   ice cream.

Jj

jack-in-the-box

Kk

kangaroo   kite

Ll

ladder   lion   library

Mm

moon

monster

motorcycle

Nn

nose

nurse

Oo

Do not   feed   (the) octopus!

Pp

parrot

piano

pirate

Qq

Where   is   (the) queen?

Rr

rocket

rain

rainbow

Ss

Can you swim?

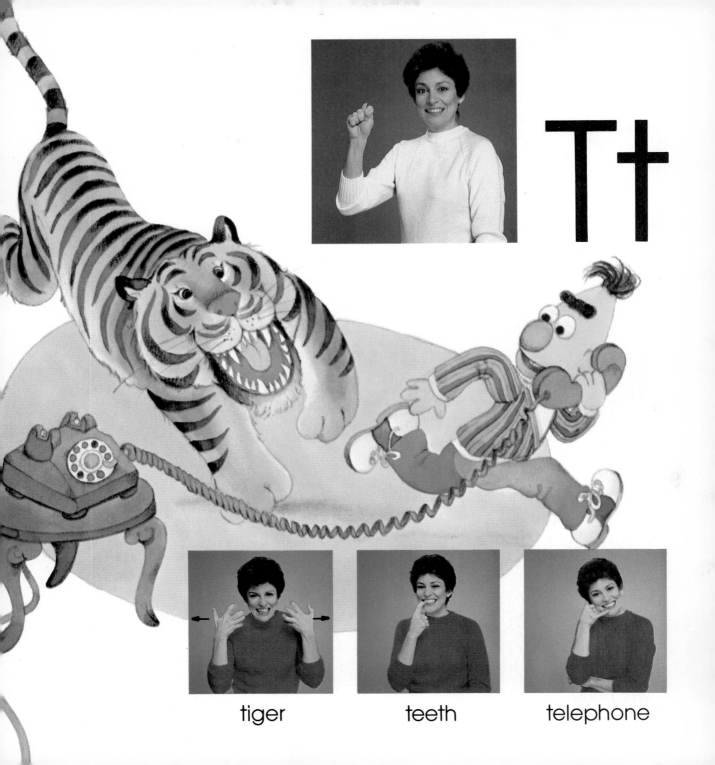

Tt

tiger

teeth

telephone

Uu

Come   under   my   umbrella.

Vv

I love you, Mommy

Will you (be) my valentine?

Ww

Who broke (the) window?

Xx

x-ray

Yy

yo-yo

Zz

zebra

Now

I

know

my

A

B

C's!